WOMEN'S EYES

WOMEN'S EYES

BEING VERSES TRANSLATED FROM THE SANSKRIT

by

Arthur William Ryder

GYAN

Published by

Gyan Publishing House
5, Ansari Road
Daryaganj, New Delhi-110002
Phone: 011-47034999, 9811692060
E-mail: books@gyanbooks.com

Distribution Network
gyanbooks.com
India, USA, Canada, UK, Australia

ISBN: 978-93-6280-029-9 (PB)
First Published, 1916

2nd Impression 2024

Printed at: Gyan Press, Delhi.

WOMEN'S EYES
Translator: ARTHUR WILLIAM RYDER

Women's Eyes

BEING VERSES TRANSLATED FROM
THE SANSKRIT

by

Arthur William Ryder

Assistant Professor of Sanskrit
in the University of California

Should fancy cease,
The world would be a forest dead and dry.
—BHAVABHUTI.

SAN FRANCISCO
A. M. ROBERTSON
1916

TO THE MEMORY OF
IRVING STRINGHAM
THE MATHEMATICIAN.
WE OF THE UNIVERSITY OWE MORE TO HIM
THAN EITHER WE COULD REPAY OR
WHOLLY COMPREHEND. TO HIS LIVING
MEMORY THIS VOLUME IS DEDICATED; A SLIGHT
GIFT, MADE RICH ONLY BY THE LOVING
AND GRATEFUL THOUGHT OF HIM,
WHICH WENT TO ITS MAKING.

The year sees many a birth and death
Of little folks like you and me:
His like has never yet drawn breath;
No future age his like will see.

FROM THE SANSKRIT.

INTRODUCTION

IN *short verses the Hindus excel. Their mastery of form, their play of fancy, their depth and tenderness of feeling, are all exquisite.*

Of the many who wrote such verses, the greatest is Bhartrihari. He lived some fifteen hundred years ago as king of Ujjain, and lived most royally, tasting the sweets of life without thought of the morrow.

At last he was roused from his carefree existence by an event which surprised and shocked him. He gave a magic fruit to a girl whom he loved. She loved another, and passed the gift on to him. He presented it to his lady-love, who in her turn loved the king. When Bhartrihari received the magic fruit from her and learned of its travels, he was disgusted with the fleeting joys of the world, gave up his kingdom, and spent the rest of his life in a cave, writing poetry. The circumstance which led to his retirement is commemorated in the following verse, reprinted by permission of the Century Magazine:

The maid my true heart loves would not my true love be;
She seeks another man; another maid loves he;
And me another maid her own true love would see:
Oh, fie on her and him and Love and HER and me!

Bhartrihari wrote three hundred verses: a hundred on the conduct of life, a hundred on love, a hundred on renunciation.

In the present collection, no less than eighty-five of the verses are taken from this master of Indian verse-writing. The remaining fifteen are from various sources. The arrangement of the verses is my own, as are also the titles prefixed to them.

I have striven faithfully for a literal rendering. Though a rendering into verse cannot be quite as close as a prose version, nothing has been wilfully added or subtracted. One matter deserves notice here; I have occasionally translated Indian god-names, Shiva or Brahma, by the word God. This is not wholly accurate, yet not, I think, unfaithful in spirit.

The present volume does not encroach unduly upon the excellent work of P. E. More: A Century of Indian Epigrams. Only a few of the verses chosen by him are translated here, and even these in a manner quite different.

I am under obligations to the University of California Chronicle for permission to reprint certain verses which first appeared in its pages.

I am under obligations to the University of California Chronicle for permission to reprint certain verses which first appeared in its pages.

ARTHUR W. RYDER

Berkeley, California,
February 19, 1910.

CONTENTS

PAGE

WOMEN'S EYES

WOMEN'S EYES

The world is full of women's eyes,
Defiant, filled with shy surprise,
Demure, a little overfree,
Or simply sparkling roguishly;
It seems a gorgeous lily-bed,
Whichever way I turn my head.

IF ONLY WE MIGHT DRESS IN AIR

If only we might dress in air,
    And eat what begging brings,
And sleep outdoors, we should not care
    For all the money-kings.

LOVE IS YOUNG

The wrinkles on my face are all untold;
My hair is gray and thin;
My limbs are sadly feeble grown, and old:
But love is young, and sin.

LOVE GROWS BY WHAT IT FEEDS ON

When she is far, I only want to see her;
  When she is seen, I only want to kiss her;
When she is kissed, I never want to flee her;
  I know that I could never bear to miss her.

GENTLE EYES

Candle, and fire, and star,
    Sun, moon, to give me light;
But her dear, gentle eyes are far—
    This world is night.

THE STUBBORN FOOL I

A diamond you may draw
From an alligator's jaw;
You may cross the raging ocean like a pool;
A cobra you may wear
Like a blossom in your hair;
But you never can convince a stubborn fool.

With sufficient toil and travail
You may gather oil from gravel;
The mirage perhaps your thirsty lips may cool;
If you seek it night and morn,
You may find a rabbit's horn;
But you never can convince a stubborn fool.

Seven arrows pierce my heart:
The moonbeams that by day depart;
The maid whose youthful beauty flies;
The pool wherein the lotus dies;
The handsome man whose lips are dumb;
The rich man, miserly and glum;
The good man sunk in suffering;
The rogue in favor with the king.

SUBSTITUTES

What need of armor to the patient soul?
What need of foes, if temper spurns control?
If rogues are near, what need of snakes to harm
you?
If relatives, what need of fire to warm you?
If friends, what need of magic draughts for
health?
If blameless scholarship, what need of wealth?
If modesty, what need of gems and flowers?
If poetry, what need of kingly powers?

SWEET AND BITTER

Sweet are the moonbeams, sweet the grass-grown
wood,
Sweet is the peaceful converse of the good,
The poet's song is sweet, the maiden's face
When angry tear-drops lend a sudden grace:
All would be sweet if human fate were fitter;
The thought of death turns all the sweet to
bitter.

WHEN I KNEW A LITTLE BIT

When I knew a little bit,
Then my silly, blinded wit,
Mad as elephants in rut,
Thought it was omnisicent; but
When I learned a little more
From the scholar's hoarded store,
Madness' fever soon grew cool,
And I knew I was a fool.

WHOM DOES SHE LOVE?

With one she gossips full of art;
    Her glances with a second flirt;
She holds another in her heart:
    Whom does she love enough to hurt?

ARROWS OF LOVE

Where are you going, winsome maid,
Through deepest, darkest night? (he said.)
I go to him whom love has made
Dearer to me than life (she said).
Ah, girl, and are you not afraid,
For you are all alone? (he said.)
The god of love shall be mine aid,
Arrows of love fly true (she said).

THE DANGER OF DELAY

In giving, and receiving too,
In every deed you have to do,
Act quickly; if you wait a bit,
Then time will suck the juice of it.

BETTER TO DWELL IN MOUNTAINS WILD

Better to dwell in mountains wild
    With beasts of prey
Than in the palaces of gods
    With fools to stay.

THE APRIL WIND

The wind of April is a lover bold:
He makes the women shiver hot and cold;
He shuts their eyes, he rumples up their hair,
And catches rudely at the gowns they wear;
Time after time he presses pretty lips
From which a cry indignant-joyful slips.

MY FOLLY 'S DONE

Why should that girl still use her keen,
Coquettish eyes that steal the sheen
From lotus-flowers. What can she mean?

My folly 's done. The fever-sting
Of love's soft arrow does not cling;
And yet she doesn't stop, poor thing!

DOES SHE LOVE ME?

Although she does not speak to me,
She listens while I speak;
Her eyes turn not, my face to see,
But nothing else they seek.

REMEDIES

A fire with water we defeat,
With parasols the midday heat,
Mad elephants with goads that prick,
Oxen and asses with a stick,
Sickness with draughts that banish harm,
Poison with many a spell and charm;
Science has cures for every ill
Except the fool; he prospers still.

You are a teacher of the youth
Who master philosophic truth;
I seek in the poetic art
What charms and ravishes the heart.
Yet we are honest and we see
The only good is charity;
And nothing charms us, fools or wise,
Except a maid with lotus-eyes.

His powers are still the same, his actions too,
His mind is quite as keen, his speech as true;
Yet he has undergone a wondrous change—
He lost his money. Do you think it strange?

DESIRE IS YOUNG

Not time, but we, have passed away;
  Not virtue, we ourselves grow cold;
Not joys, but we, no longer stay:
  Desire is young, but we are old.

THOU ART A FLOWER

Thou art a flower whose fragrance none has
 tasted,
 A gem uncut by workman's tool,
A branch no desecrating hands have wasted,
 A virgin forest, sweetly cool.

No man on earth deserves to taste thy beauty,
 Thy blameless loveliness and worth,
Unless he has fulfilled man's perfect duty—
 And is there such a one on earth?

Thy wise creator wrote upon thy brow,
    When thou wast born, what wealth should
        once be thine;
The sum was great perhaps, or small; yet now
    Thy fate is fixed, and sure the law divine.

For if thou dwell within the desert's bound,
    Thou shalt have nothing less than his decree;
Nor shall a single penny more be found,
    Although the golden mount thy dwelling be.

Ah, then be brave and play the manly part,
Nor be so fond to humble thy proud heart
And fawn before the rich with cringing art.

For see! A jar that in the ocean fell
Holds no more water in its little shell
Than when you lowered it in the meanest well.

TWO KINGS

Flee from the palace where they say:
The king is sleeping; go away—
He has no time for you today—
Or—he will see you if you stay—
He will be angry anyway.

Flee to another, greater king,
My soul, who rules each mortal thing,
Whose palace knows no bolt, no ring,
No porter's harsh, sarcastic fling,
No pain, no human suffering.

ABSENCE AND UNION

Absence is union dear,
 When hearts are one;
Union is absence drear,
 When love is done.

THE SERPENT-WOMAN

Avoid the poison-glance, my friends;
The serpent-woman flee;
Her crooked path has crooked ends;
Her hood is coquetry.

If you are stung by common snakes,
Perhaps you will not die;
If poison from a woman takes,
The doctors say goodby.

CAN SHE BE DEAR?

The thought of her is saddening,
The sight of her is fear,
The touch of her is maddening—
Can she be really dear?

THE DECLINE OF TRUE LEARNING

Once, learning slew the living woe
Of wise men. That was long ago.
She then disdained such service rare,
Became a practical affair.
But nowadays she sees that kings
Despise all intellectual things,
And sinking lower day by day,
She seems to vanish quite away.

THE LAST DAY

When the celestial mount shall totter, burning
In all-devouring flame,
When seas go dry, where crocodiles are turning
And sharks no man may tame,
When the compact earth itself shall tumble sheer,
Great mountains madly dance,
What of our bodies, quivering like the ear
Of baby elephants?

LOGIC

How long may subtle logic play its part
In science and theology and art?
    So long as no young fawn-eyed maiden's glance
Shall find its way to the logician's heart.

None from the anger of the king
  May be released;
The fire consumes the offering
  And burns the priest.

THE RAINS

And when the rainy days are come,
Your lady-love must stay at home;
She clings to you, a little bold
Because she shivers with the cold;
The breeze is fresh with heaven's spray
And drives her lassitude away:
When happy lovers are together,
The rainy time is fairest weather.

THE LOVERS' ALLY

Ye maids, exhaust your haughty scorn
On lovers bending low;
For soon the breeze in southland born,
With sandal sweet, will blow.

WHY?

The deer, the fish, the good man hunger
  For grass, for water, for content;
Yet hunter, fisher, scandalmonger
  Pursue each harmless innocent.

Child for an hour, and lovesick youth an hour,
  Beggar an hour, then fanned by riches' breath,
The wrinkled actor, Man, bereft of power,
  Creeps tottering behind the curtain, Death.

In daily journeys of the sun
Our little life is quickly done;
In anxious duties of the day
The hours unnoticed slip away;
Though birth and age are ever near,
And grief, and death, we do not fear:
The world forgets its sore distress,
Goes mad with wine of heedlessness.

SHE ONLY LOOKED

She did not redden nor deny
  My entrance to her room;
She did not speak an angry word;
  She did not fret and fume;
She did not frown upon poor me,
  Her lover now as then;
She only looked at me the way
  She looks at other men.

WHO UNDERSTANDS A MAN?

Once he would follow at my feet,
  Obey my slightest word;
And black was black, if black to me,
  Or white, if I preferred;
And he began to walk or sit
  The moment I began;
But he is different now. Oh, dear!
  Who understands a man?

UNTRUSTWORTHY THINGS

The things that can claw, and the things that
 can gore,
 Are very untrustworthy things;
And a man with a sword in his hand, further-
 more,
 And rivers and women and kings.

TWO VIEWS OF LIFE

When ignorance my life entwined,
Love's ointment made me strangely blind—
I thought the world was made of womankind.

But clearer judgment than of yore
The veil before my vision tore—
I know that God is all the world and more.

PROCRASTINATION

By and by—
Never fret—
I shall try
By and by.

By and by—
Don't forget—
You must die
By and by.

SHOULD FANCY CEASE

The lover's patient fancy brings him peace,
  Paints her he loves before his inward eye,
And gives him comfort; but should fancy cease,
  The world would be a forest dead and dry,
  And hearts that shrivel in the burning chaff,
    must die.

WHAT THEN? I

What if my life is fed
  With all that seems most sweet?
What if my foeman's head
  Is ground beneath my feet?
What if my wealth makes friends
  Again and yet again?
What if my soul ascends
  Through countless lives? What then?

WHAT THEN? II

Old rags, or fine, white silk that flows and clings—
  Why should I care?
Poor wife, or horses, elephants, and things—
  What difference there?
Sweet rice, or wretched food when day is o'er—
  Why care again?
God's light, or groping in the dark once more—
  What then? What then?

THE QUEEN OF LOVE

Surely the love-god is the slave
    Of her sweet eyes;
For when they give a hint, the knave
    Obedient flies.

JOYOUS TREASURES

How hard a thing it is that they achieve
Whose hearts the thought of God keeps pure
and bright,
Who for His sake earth's joyous treasures leave
Without a pang at losing such delight!

Those joyous treasures I could never get;
I cannot get them now; I am not sure
That I shall ever win to them; and yet
I cannot flout the thought, the hope, the lure.

VEXATIONS I

The scholarship that grasps at straws,
    The woman's love that must be bought,
The life that hangs on tyrants' laws—
    These things are with vexation fraught.

VEXATIONS II

The fear of dying vexes birth;
  Age vexes flashing youth;
The carper vexes honest worth;
  Irresolution, truth.

To vex our peace the women love;
  Our joy, ambition's sting;
Rogues vex the court, and snakes the grove;
  And something, everything.

LOVE, THE FISHER

Love, the fisher, casts his woman-hook
    Into the sea of lust and fond desire,
And just as soon as greedy men-fish look
    And snap the red bait, lips so sweet, so dire,
Then he is quick to catch them and to cook
    The hungry wretches over passion's fire.

If mouths are dry with thirst,
Men think of water first;
If hungry, bolt their rice
With many a toothsome spice;
If love flames bright and brighter,
They clasp the women tighter:
They have the strangest notions;
They think ephemeral potions
Will heal the soul's commotions.

What though she have a bosom sweet,
    A form to beauty wed,
A face in which the graces meet—
    She must not turn your head.

Nay, if her charm your fancy haunts,
    Then live on virtue's food;
One cannot have the things he wants
    Except by being good.

THE BLIND FOREST

The lady's body is a forest blind,
    With dangerous hills, her bosom fair;
Think not to wander there, my mind;
    The robber, Love, is lurking there.

THE LITTLENESS OF THE WORLD

Why should the truly wise man wish
  To hold the world in fee?
'T is but the leaping of a baby fish
  Upon the boundless sea.

FRIENDSHIP'S END

Yes, you were I, and I was you,
So fond the love that linked us two;
Alas, my friend, for friendship's end!
Now I am I, and you are you.

A WASTED LIFE I

No stainless wisdom have I learned;
No honest money have I earned;
No fond obedience have I brought
To parents, with a heart well-taught;
I never dreamed of sweet embraces,
Of sparkling eyes and roguish faces:
My life was wasted like the crow's;
I lived on strangers' bread and blows.

I never learned to vanquish other men
In conference, with the just and fitting word;
I never made high heaven ring again,
Praising the elephant-hunter's sturdy sword;
I never tasted honey from the kind,
Soft lips of maids when moonlight scatters gloom:
My youth is gone and left no good behind,
A candle burning in an empty room.

A WASTED LIFE III

The paths of thought I never trod
Which lead to unity in God;
Nor were my days to virtue given
Which opens wide the gates of heaven;
Delights of love that men esteem
Were mine not even in a dream:
I was a sorry axe in sooth
To cut the tree, my mother's youth.

FLAMING BANNERS

Learning and dignity,
  Wisdom and manners
Last till the god of love
  Plants flaming banners.

You practise theft by strangest arts
Once and again;
In broad daylight you steal the hearts
Of waking men.

TWO KINDS OF FRIENDSHIP

The friendship of the rogue or saint,
Like shade at dawn or shade at noon,
Starts large and slowly grows more faint,
Or starting faint, grows larger soon.

CHOOSING A VOCATION

What shall I do in these few hours of life?
Live humbly with a sweet, religious wife?
Renounce the world, the ties of kindred sever,
And spend my days beside the sacred river?
Drink deep of honeyed poems' nectar-flow?
Or learn philosophy? I hardly know.

THE GOOD ARE RARE

Through thoughts and words and deeds their
    virtues flow;
  To all the world their kindness brings delight;
They make a mote of good in others show
  Like a great mountain; for their hearts are
    bright,
And brighten all they touch with their own worth:
How many such are to be found on earth?

THERE WAS A NOBLE CITY

There was a noble city old,
A mighty king, and vassals bold;
And there were gathered scholars true,
And moon-faced ladies not a few;
And there were princes proud and free,
And stories told, and minstrelsy:
A memory now; we mourn their fall
And honor Time, who levels all.

WHERE EDUCATION FAILS

Though many youths a training get
In law, religion, etiquette,
Why are there few whose actions would,
Interpreted, seem wholly good?

Some arching brow is sure to be
As cunning as a master-key,
That serves its purpose passing well
In flinging wide the gates of hell.

A girl is held in trust, another's treasure;
To arms of love my child today is given;
And now I feel a calm and sacred pleasure;
I have restored the pledge that came from
heaven.

STRUGGLING FANCIES

It is my body leaves my love, not I;
  My body moves away, but not my mind;
For back to her my struggling fancies fly
  Like silken banners borne against the wind.

OH, MIGHT I END THE QUEST!

I dug beneath the earth most greedily
    In search of hidden treasure;
I smelted ore; I crossed the mighty sea,
    Forgetting every pleasure;
I cringed to kings; and muddling all my brains
    With magic, lost my rest:
But never got a penny for my pains;
    Oh, might I end the quest!

WHAT DELIGHTS AND HURTS

It is the truth sans prejudice I speak;
Ye people, heed this truth forever true;
All that delights, in women you must seek,
And all that hurts, you find in women too.

THE SWEETEST THINGS

The sweetest sight a man may see
Is a maiden's loving face;
The sweetest thing to touch should be
Her body's close embrace;

Her voice should be the sweetest sound;
Her breath, the sweetest scent;
The sweetest taste, the honey found
On lips to kisses lent;

The thought of her is fervent prayer,
Religion's sweetest part;
The charm of her is everywhere
Unto the pure in heart.

THE UNLUCKY MAN

A bald man once, whose hairless pate
    Felt inconveniently hot,
Fled to a cocoa-tree at noon—
    He hoped to find a shady spot.
And then a big nut fell, and crack!
    The poor bald head was split in two.
Misfortunes almost always find
    The man whom evil fates pursue.

A REASON FOR RENUNCIATION

Possessions leave us at the end,
  However long they stay;
Then why not cast aside, my friend,
  What leaves us anyway?

And if they leave against our will,
  The heart takes time in mending;
If given willingly, they fill
  That heart with joy unending.

RENUNCIATION

What does renunciation mean?
It means a lonely woodland scene
Remote from men and human sin,
From woes of love, from love of kin,
Free from the world, a life apart
That slays the tortures of the heart
As fear of death and fear of birth:
It means the best of heaven and earth.

Is there no splendid Himalayan height,
    Cooled by the spray from Ganges' holy springs
With rocks where fairies now and then alight,
    That men should fawn upon contemptuous
        kings?

"Here are banquets, and singing sweet,
Perfumes, and glimpse of dancing feet,
And bosoms that on mine may beat."

Five rascal senses whisper this,
Lead me from virtue much amiss,
And cheat me of my highest bliss.

WHEN WOMAN WILLS

When loving woman wants her way,
God hesitates to say her nay.

A LITTLE KNOWLEDGE

A fool's opinion easily is bent;
    More easy 't is to win the wise and great;
But God himself could never make content
    The man who feels himself elate
    With one small grain of knowledge in his
        pate.

THE WEAKER SEX

The classic poets make a great mistake;
  Forever of the weaker sex they speak;
When gods are subjugated for the sake
  Of starry glances, are the women weak?

Half-smiles that brighten on her face,
Innocent, roving glances,
The wealth of budding charms that show
In little steps and dances,
The flow of words that shyly prove
The sweet, new woman-feeling:
Yes, all the fawn-eyed maiden does
Is wondrously appealing.

THE BRAVEST OF THE BRAVE

A few brave men pursue
  Rogue elephants to death;
There are a braver few
  Who stop the lion's breath;
The bravest of the brave—
  And fewer yet they prove—
Are they who can enslave
  The haughty god of love.

DIGNITY

The dog will roll, and wag his tail, and fawn,
Show mouth and belly, just to get some meat;
The majestic elephant gazes gravely on;
Till coaxed a hundred times, he will not eat.

IN THE DAYS OF THY YOUTH

While life is vigorous and bright,
While sickness comes not, nor decay,
While all your powers are at their height,
While yet old age is far away,
Then, wise man, let your thoughts be turning
To heaven's hopes and fears of hell;
For when the house is fired and burning,
It is too late to dig a well.

THEY WANT THE EARTH

'T is but a little ball of mud
With a streak of water round;
Yet kings for it will shed their blood,
As for a treasure found.

They cannot, will not leave the thing,
So poor are they, so mean;
And men will fawn on such a king!
Oh, shame upon the scene!

THE BEASTS THAT DON'T EAT GRASS

Unschooled in music, poetry, and art,
  Man is a beast, a hornless, tailless beast;
  He doesn't eat the grass; for this at least
The other beasts may well be glad at heart.

WHY MEN BEG

Is there a man of spirit who would beg
    In broken words that stumble with his sobbing,
Harsh sobs of him who fears a surly "no!"
    And all to ease his belly's empty throbbing?

None but the man who sees his wretched wife
    Sad always, sees her worn and ragged skirts,
Sees sad-faced babies tugging at their folds
    With screams that tell how fiercely hunger
        hurts.

THE WISE MISOGYNIST

The wise misogynist, poor soul,
To self-deceit is given;
For heaven rewards his self-control,
And women swarm in heaven.

NECTAR AND POISON

All nectar and all poison lives
In woman's changing states;
For she is nectar when she loves,
And poison when she hates.

THE TWO THINGS THAT MATTER

Why all this talk and foolish chatter?
There are just two things that really matter:
A buxom, young, and frisky wife;
Or else a lonely forest-life.

THE ONE THING NEEDFUL

Why should I study scripture, sacred lore,
Or any good, big book? Why get a store
Of pious actions, anxiously performed—
And win a humble tent in heaven, no more?

The knowledge of myself is all I need
To give me lasting joy, to burn the seed
Of the interminable pain of life—
Let pious peddlars show their wares and plead.

Are palace-joys so incomplete?
  Is song a despicable pleasure?
And is there anything so sweet
  As clasping her you love and treasure?

Yet pious men account these things
  As vain as flickering candle-light
'Neath dancing moths on troubled wings;
  And to the woods they take their flight.

THE LINES OF FATE

If thorn-plants in the desert leafless be,
    The spring is not to blame.
If owls in broadest daylight cannot see,
    The sun should feel no shame.
If in the plover's bill no raindrops fall,
    'T were wrong to blame the cloud.
The lines that fate has written once for all,
    Are never disallowed.

POVERTY

The moon by night, the sun by day
Continue in their heavenly way;
One rag they have, one ragged cloud
To serve them both as robe and shroud.
Poor things!

HOW HARD FATE GRIPS!

The snake and elephant are caged;
The moon and sun must meet eclipse;
The prudent are in strife engaged
With poverty. How hard fate grips!

WHEN MY LOVE DRAWS NIGH

When my love draws nigh,
  When his voice I hear,
Why am I all eye?
  Why am I all ear?

THE HERMIT

I seem to see a hermit good:
He has no pride, he begs his food;
From man-made laws his acts are free;
He seeks no man's society;
He has no care for common ways
Of giving, getting all his days;
He stitches up his garment ragged
With wayside tatters, torn and jagged;
No false conceit his fancy haunts—
Eternal peace is all he wants.

WHY GO TO COURT?

I am not fashion's changing sport,
  I never acted, sang, nor hated;
What figure should I cut at court?
  I am no lady languid-gaited.

IMPOSSIBLE!

The consecrated saints of eld
  Who lived on water, leaves, and air,
Went mad with love when they beheld
  A face that showed how maids are fair.

And if the common men who eat
  Their rice and milk and curds and ghee,
Should curb the wish for things so sweet,
  The mountains would fly oversea.

HINDRANCES

'T would not be hard, through life's gray sea
    To find the track;
But fawn-eyed women hinder me,
    And hold me back.

DIVINE VISION

My love is in a distant land,
And yet I see her where I stand.
The gods have vision less divine,
Because the eye of love is mine.

WHY MY POEMS DIED

The critics all were jealous,
The patrons full of pride,
The public had no judgment;
And so my poems died.